# *According to Sand*

PRAISE FOR THE POETRY OF THORPE MOECKEL

"…a striking and original book of poems. It has the fresh, raw taste of a wilderness river."

—Jim Harrison, author of *Dead Man's Float*

"Thorpe Moeckel is a litanist, pilgrim, sensualist, beseecher, explorer, and connoisseur of the heart's underbrush and waterways."

—Lisa Russ Spaar, author of *Madrigalia*

"Moeckel's generosity shines through his poems, and his awareness, modest and keen as a knife-edge, sometimes makes me shiver with delight."

—David Young, author of *Field of Light and Shadow*

## MORE BOOKS BY THE AUTHOR

*Odd Botany*

*Making a Map of the River*

*Venison*

*Watershed Days*

*Arcadia Road: A Trilogy*

*Down by the Eno, Down by the Haw: A Wonder Almanac*

## CHAPBOOKS

*Meltlines*

*The Guessing Land*

*Off Owl's Head*

# *According to Sand*

POEMS

THORPE MOECKEL

MERCER UNIVERSITY PRESS
*Macon, Georgia*

MUP/ P651


Published by Mercer University Press
1501 Mercer University Drive
Macon, Georgia 31207


26 25 24 23 22     5 4 3 2 1

Books published by Mercer University Press are printed on acid-free paper that meets the requirements of the American National Standard for Information Sciences—Permanence of Paper for Printed Library Materials.

Printed and bound in the UNITED STATES.

This book is set in ADOBE CASLON PRO.

Cover/jacket design by BURT&BURT.

ISBN 978-0-88146-857-1

Cataloging-in-Publication Data is available from the Library of Congress

*for my sister, Sydney Buppert,*
*and her family,*

*and for my brother, James*

MERCER UNIVERSITY PRESS

*Endowed by*

TOM WATSON BROWN

*and*

THE WATSON-BROWN FOUNDATION, INC.

# CONTENTS

*According to Sand*

# SOUTH SWELL

Last night's moon-voodoo,
the sun with its amber eggs –

this is origin's breakfast.
The books of the seers are burning,

so continent, so effulgent.

Each wave is a fracture.
Each wave is a gush & an ambassador of grace.

They flick you off, do your Tai Chi.
They roll a glaze.

They don't you.

# PALEOZOIC FOLK SONG

And there, over there, is a doll's head
among the branches that only branch
                    to the edge of the flood;
it has a face
on either side of its skull. Again

its glances save me, and from what

is not what the beech leaves rattle for,
strange bugles. Speak of the river, doll, say

it has a secret. *It has no secret*

ꝺ

says one face, the sleeping one. The hair
is a dreadlocks
of silt, remnant of those stones that gave birth

            to the extinctions. *It does*,
says doll's stunned, wakeful face,
*have a secret*,

*but only the trees have known enough*
*to forget it clearly:*

*ask them*. See,

ꝺ

there's a hollow in the sand the size
of the hole where

doll's head once attached
to a body, now gone. So I stick the head
by that hole on a small, vertical member
of the truck's ladder rack and ask it
to keep quiet
and sing. For miles,

though they are not ages anymore,

the river follows. Everywhere
I look—
for a pulse, a sinew—
there is no homesickness

again. No necks either,
only water & stones
of light,
and trees where the water

wears the stones to trees.

# THE AUGUST LISTENER

But I was trying to think in bug time,
as though a day was a season and a season was a life.

For instance, it was Saturday,
humidity flat-lined & flush,
some lather, more drool. Gullied.
The clay-matrix damp, frenetic stillness of roots

tangled, a post-flow affair. I mean the ambient,
I mean a blister nuthatch gnawed at.

Not
a drill, August's language, but a pupa. I touched
my forehead, there—& knew it.

❧

Woodwind, pincher, antsoul.
Or this: skimmer & glide,
glissando & shimmer—
summer's music,

scoops of rice in a paper bag. It entered me
like a sleeping breath, not quite lungful,
nourishing all the same, sun on skin, skin
on water; the clouds gladiolaed & close,

damselfly's air traffic: the vectors, the orbits,
the thrift.

❧

Toward afternoon & catbird preened from the edge
                    of something, forgetting
maybe, or lassitude. But there was a girl making
          a spongeball of scum at the edge of the pond,
her arms like slivers of moon. *I'm going*
*to throw it in the water,* she said,
                                        *and see what it does.*
At once, green heron began a song
like knocking
on wood.

❧

If sweetness had a sound,
                              and sweetness had a sound,
it dipped my heart in summer's butter
          a while. Well,
it did. It fried me good.

❧

Because the air had let go
of emptiness, because folly's a hard sell

in such a groove, because even the soil settling
had a rhythm beneath hearing. Or because the frogs
needed to boot up like that. Like that.

Or because they didn't and belief's a kind of headphones. But more
likely because it's a girdle, no, a corset of sweat & light.

❧

in pairs, or in funnels of three, as if in chase,
the dragonflies stirred summer's soup. I doubt they meant to,
or even sensed
the haze where webs clammed like loss & finding
in the ur-radiance, juicing
the phloem anyway. Then the rasp
and hoofthump of whitetails: said *listen*,
said *go*.

❧

Sweetgum fruit a gleamworks of nub & flay,
nearly neon with wantjuice, as when skink flitted
like seeing out of seeing, a tailwhip into crevice—

and so each night by the pond the chorus began.

❧

Butterfly
on buttonbush, the pond a green glaze. I didn't mean
to be hugged. I didn't want one more thing,
not the chalksplotches
of blossoms on the far shore,

not the pine fallen across the cove, its scales or
the brown needles still
on the branch. But the whirr
and skitch, I'd take that, and the birds' bubbles & rouge,
their lime. Yes, color to make me blind.

~

So the ears

grew eyes and ceased to sweat. How amphibious even
          the sky in its slow fade, lavender to taupe, blueberries

and ream. As if each day, too, the world fluffed its pillow.
          Yes, in wanting nothing, I wanted more. You see,

I wanted nothing but the slow pulse of evening,
cantata of katydids, the frogs saying *this, this, this*.

And the bats, then, to hear like a bat.

# THE GUESSING LAND

1

My goo, it stun prey & predator,
a mode of travel, expendable legs.
This life: endless slithering—
much thick, much carnal—now
in starlight like animate drool.

## 2

What do we see that you call these eyes?
We succor the light: fire pink, wart-strange.
More like mouths, last night we sang
in quarter moonlight. Unheard, we began.
You were planting, burying us
in castles of manure & soil,
a swath between the peach & pear trees,
rented land. Knee shuffling, combing rows,
your hands went earth. You turned to rain.
The trance & the music were the same.

### 3

Look for us on antler, stone, wood,
certain bugs' backs.

Of us, they say:
*Annie Algae met Freddy Fungus*
*and they took a liking.*

But we say it was less
complicated than that.

4

Are skies
blue cannot enter,
economies of swell,
want-engine, utter
process. How swift
our rivers, how
silent our J & generous
with resistance.

5

We comb the shades, everywhere, dogmatic,
8-wheel drive, all lust & appetite—so many
this summer: through wheezes of grey clouds
suffused in violet's underhues,
in the lupine & first blue iris—
ascending grass blade, falling, thirsting on.

## 6

I'm looking for, I'm what to do next,
a child on roller skates for the first time—
suckerpunch, cloud-exhaust. I sky:
am ocean, am ice.

The sun is my shepherd. Am plural,
a brain-fart, a bleach.
Like hair, like the impulse to run
your fingers through it. Like this.

7

You watched me without saying a word.
How could you have spoken? Not even
the tremolo of that creek matched
my noise. Now you speak. It's useless,
I'm too much: source, absence, blockage—
sorcery, seance, cage. How else?
You never knew how easy light could be
until you tripped with me—
I undermind. You think I am
the light, and the light, that which I make
or makes me, is dark—maybe so.
Let my blank tonnage, my impalpable
scald you the answer with its coal.

1. slug 2. potatoes 3. lichen 4. cloud 5. tick 6. wind 7. shadow

# TAKING IT EASY, TAKING IT SLOW

Meanwhile, delirium chases minnows up the tupelo.

And here's the gravelly flatulence of a heron's call.
And here are mergansers, two drakes & a hen,
off the hummock's eastmost,
                                        as if born there.

But that guy there, don't mind him

lying on his sleeping bag among the cypress trees:
he's getting in touch with his inner gnome.
          See the mistletoe, natty & parasitic, little green explosions
giving suck. Water here

                                    is a dark chocolate,
and wood is wood, a little corky perhaps, a little twisted too.
Five days of swamp travel, a canoe
for home. Don't worry

                                    now, all he's going to do
is lie around a while,
let the sun cover him with its amber quilt; later

he'll get a fire going, let the big questions bring him coffee
in a blossoming red maple mug.

# PRAYER FLAGS

Goldenrod, ironweed, yarrow, thistle—
it's September,
but isn't it always September in the mist
over the valley
                                        that births the sun.
Here the clouds pluck every feather, gust
me undersky. World's over the top.

❧

Like meadow goldfish, the jewelweed—
yellow mostly, phalanged & chambered.
Call it a pollen mouth, a cave.
Are scraggly, composite-frilled,
                                                                the other flowers,
and that's fine.
The butterflies don't mind. The wind likes them too.

❧

Red-tailed over the trees, steadying
its path with twists
of rump. Over the Fraser firs. Over
the hardpan, the sharp-wired cursive
                                                                        of locust rails strung
to fence. A brief caress over
the cutover ridge, a flap & skyward arc.

❧

I've been walking hunger's puppet,
taking its pulse. Too many strings for so few

fingers—it's a scurry, a divination,
such jointwork, almost
                                        translucent:

haze-swimmer, marrowless lurch & frisson.
No bridle, but a saddlery of wind.

☙

If the passion that leathers
the burdock, that mosaic of veins at ash's trunk,
thickens the vulnerable,
let it be slow, let it
                                        —sweet demolishment—
be quiet & thorough, known
to others before, if ever to me.

☙

What September whips into shape
is splendor, mercy's migration with the storms.
So few pinks nowadays, fewer reds
in the blossoms anyway.
                                        Fruit's another story,
leaves the narrator, as untrustworthy
as true.

☙

East wind a steady lecture
on shadows & shine, clouds bearing fast fruit
over ridges, birds, trees.
Need loses me. The woods
                                        at field's edge
hear me out. So gently hectic.
So hide & seek.

# FIGURE DRAWN ON THE GROUND AS THE BULL MOOSE URINATES UPON WAKING

One must not overlook the trace marks, strayest,
or the leach tree in full radar. How

                    the unforeseen trails, leading, grooves a nest
among villas of salvage
                                                    where gleaning is melt,

a spool of vine & slather. Spiraling
even so, splashchips swallowing nuthatch,

          its whawhawant, its cling & vlirp. Meanwhile—

rear tined, bore buttered—some forever unsilences
in wiregrass tongues. But who seeks to divide

so as to nourish? Who, so as to hide, grinds
ought for worms to cast? There,
                                                              in the peninsulas.

Evidence as a molten weaning. Once
we had known the eighth kind

of starting over from seed.

## THAW

Worrying the snow that goes
sun-struck from pine, bright
while squirrel claws oak's gray
edge, I scratch my carrot-nose,
cinch my coat against the warmth. What
I need is what I fear: to learn
not to melt, not to freeze too hard.

Crow lands on my head and bellows
in that awful voice of his—such fright!—
"if you bleed water, say,
and my blood is the blood of shadows,
then what do you weep, what—
winter's purple?" "No," I squeak, seeing farmer
aim. "Crow blood, of being so forward."

Warmth makes me and warmth undoes.
So while it's possible, I court
the shadows—what other way?—
all that's flat: the sun's lows,
inversions of smoke. Still, to sit
shrinking, my inside feels reborn,
as if body was breath and centered.

Who shivers touches me, who grows
plants that blossom at night,

licks metal, and on a frigid day
runs naked, inhaling to whistle. Whose
favorite color is ice and favorite
shape is round, yes, who rides the Northern,
prefers the drowned over the charred.

❧

The land doesn't speak to me; it knows
I'm what it says. Dusklight,
water's ways—it could be May;
I'm going, going fast. Such prose
warmth is. Earlier the child gave me fat
strands of ivy for locks. Then wonder,
that strange thing, tied them in a braid.

❧

Warm sun again; I'm slick with flows.
Always, in such thaws, I grow polite
remembering rivers. Odor of clay,
cedar, root—this branching, towards rose,
stone, where motion—elegant bat—
is stillness, and elsewhere
worry's wind: will, surrendered.

❧

Three parts, none the same—potatoes,
that easy. Child packed me tight,
knew stains made me pure: hay,
muck, leaf, coal for eyes, a nose.
No winter brain, not that:
she began with a flake, added one more
then another, and so on, outward.

# OLD DOG

It seemed to grow us tails, it seemed
to make us wag them

each time he took a blade or two of grass—
he licks, the snaps of jaw—

then sat again or sniffed a minute, and laid downand
began to pant,

and glanced over the creek, maybe at the butterflies
in the blossoming weeds, or at

the water's double in the light on the leaves,
his abdomen rising

and falling in time with the dove coo & the train,
and sometimes his head

was flat on the ground, earth at chin-level,
or he lifted it and sniffed,

licked his paw or snapped at a bee, maybe standing again,
maybe adding a line

to that song, you know, the one you're breathing,
the one you're standing on, singing.

# WEST FORK OF THE LITTLE

So flesh comes to this: hawkweed & monarch,
   sweetflag in clumps, densities of ochre,
new vowels up from cutbank's loam, some dot
   to dot the eyes trace to spell a way into
flame azalea, pink azalea, laurel buds,
   so many, about to burst. Bless, double,
the startled raccoon, the eight wood ducks
   taking off. Goldfinch, hermit thrush,
how flowering blackberries unbramble the dusk.
   And bless this breath, the next. Each rill
and mewl, cohosh's glances, trillium in fruit,
   the gash & gush of a tributary entering
under black locust, brief flurry of blossoms
   in the breeze, spring's plunder & wheeze.

# DIX ISLAND SERENADE

Time is long with listening. Night longer.
Gulls, throatsore with beauty, jack up
even the foghorn's snoring. Forget
what edge of tongue
they sand,
bespruced one; your eyes are racy
that way, each a barnacle

hungry for sleeptides, clinging. Meanwhile
the moon clothespins this burnpile
to the daisy's innermost. And you watch,
urchin

succulently barbed. What's seen
is little blue people hoteling in ledge,
wonder hauling off its punt,
the cardinal points mouth to mouth. God,

there's too much. Cormorants open
their oils to the south. Astonishments
tinkle in the rocks. With each surge, keen
to smooch wavelips. But wings

are questions whose froth frosts the wrack,
quarries the remains. Nothing is leveled out
Even so,
insatiables collide. Every rock
is a river again,

waves turns pink before breaking. There's rejoice
clapping its hands on ledge. Lichen, those thumbprints of becoming,
have stolen the X from ecstatic. It's cute

how insistence denies itself,
the mussels' shyness, pegmatite,
orthoclase. But heapage, dear, won't you swim
in the fritillaries of morning's elbow. At least,

speak of the revenant that weaves marriage
and dismay. You are always learning here
that suffer is its own release, that talon
is fishspine's ghost. But who teaches
that clarify and understand

are butter, are
render?

## FROM THE BOW AND STERN

You were kneeling in the cove, and while between the water
and your knees was a canoe, layers of epoxy & fiber,
above as a whistling bullet a black duck

shot for the edge of the trees, which reached like
any good trees beyond their edges; and there was
a rhythm involving the dip and then the purchase

of the blade, a hip-swivel and another dip & press
of the wooden paddle's blade; and you were thoughtless,
the mind reaching like branches reflected

on dusklit water, as far down as up. No wind,
and the clouds were loblollied—indigo, licorice.
Soon there'd be a moon in this journey of stasis

and motion, and as you drifted, laid the paddle askance
gunwale, duck gone, you remembered a silence
that hadn't tried to be quiet or coy or colorless,

in which even the darkness shone, raw as mist—
a silence so simple that now the heron's blear,
the maple, lupine shoots, and alder rose

in your eye as though you'd never bear
the same rain twice; and the moon was there,
just there, further than where the duck had been,

east & inward too, and you were breathing again,
holding the paddle again, and with a softer touch,
knowing lichen, the heady mellowness of birch.

# AVIAN DISJECTA

Splurd of heron crap      on sycamore leaf
  half submerged near      the scum-gummed edge

of a drainage low      with days so dust smeared
  rattlers thick as legs      blow their covers each

morning as mist bursts      more downy than minds
  moist with much having—      there's such heron in

this nucleus-vague      nexus of gloss, such
  flight, pale-slow light   in this sprayzone-flecked

perimeter, one      wonders since when
  wasn't the palette      the art, pattern the heart.

# FATHER ON THE BEACH, TIDE COMING IN

One wave breaking, another spreading thin
like flesh under lasers, under radiation:
cells begin, end, and begin again.
Now you're in shallow with my toddler twins,
sandcastle giggles and wonderful grins—
another wave breaking, one reaching thin

as the glide and veer of the sixth pelican
coming over the dunes against the wind.
It's true. Things begin, end, begin again:
clots in your leg, hat with huge brim,
your second marriage a cool summer wind
(one wave broken, another standing trim).

Because joy's a tumble and grief's a spin
of end and begin and end again,
in salt old man this note I'll send:
how family is family and rarely cleansed,
some waves breaking, others spreading thin
that love begin, end, and begin again.

## FOG MULL

He knew that water had a plan.
Not to think

was best, he thought.
The compass said eighty degrees.
He wanted

to believe the compass,
but islands rose in the ocean
of his ears.
Slowly

he loosened his grip
on the throttle, bent his knees

as his mother used to do
when she worked in the kitchen—
wine in one hand, sponge
in the other. Where the horizon should have been,

she stood—knit shirt, shorts—
holding a plate

with apple sauce, green beans,
and ham. Somewhere
he heard the prop, its weed-slick blade,

slap of chop on the hull
like the sound of gulls
half irritable, half ecstatic.
          "Would you like

milk tonight," she asked,
"or water?

# ON HEARING THE WATERTHRUSH AGAIN, JEFFERSON

*March 1794*

ordered a Nebbiolo, briskmost vintage,
to be fetched from the cellar;
ordered Lilly, their overseer,

to deliver the canal men
an extra whiskey ration by
the same cart, mule-drawn, that hauled

the grindstone, spare tools. See,
the dogwood petals were beginning
to drop, and hickory's fires flared dusk

wilder than the day's measures
of rain, last storm a gusty pelting
around five, followed by blue

in breaks like waking. Walking,
he'd heard parula, cardinal, spooked
a blue winged teal (pale whorl of its face),

countless geese, turtles, a green heron,
wood ducks in pairs. *My fits of head-ache*
that dawn he'd inked *have stuck some days*

*hours*. Stingers, still. Yes, everything reeked
of abundance, the strafe & groan beneath
all growth, banks a forge where blossoms

were sparks rising from that hammer
no hand ever bears. Even the river—
siltslappy Rivanna—seemed to have grown

wings, a throat lusty and coarse. He heard
molt. Heard vowels, their origins, too,
but knew only the lost could follow such

speech, if speech, and turned for home.

# COLD RANGE, HOT RANGE

We're at the Potts Mountain Shooting Range
on a hot day in March, blowing ammo,
hosing the shale. Submachine, .357,
Glock. And to pepper fine holes

in the paper target, an assault shotgun
that holds eight shells. It's wild
as fire to play with fire. I like it,
fear it. Pressure in the gut, tremors

ear to marrow. Each cone of flame,
the burnt powder's sweetness & stench.
Down the line a man sights in
a .50 caliber muzzleloader,

all smoke & ear protection. Cold range,
the .22 shooter shouts, questioning.
Cold range, we reply, and check again
the guy with the .308, the bald one

with the aught six, before heading
to gather, change targets, boots
crunching brass. It's the velocity,
perfectly invisible & close,

more timeless than timelessness.
And the potency—almost innocent—
of one gentle finger squeeze.
And how each time the dust flies,

thirty rounds of nine mil out
the MP5, I'm amazed to be
breathing still. Out there I tell
my demons to dance. I don't ask

for final words. This is serious,
lucky, crazy. And maybe
some of us are aiming less
at the target's inner circle,

strange whirlpool, than at the itch—
everywhere, nowhere—to hold the barrel
to the mouth's gummy roof. If
suicide's the only serious question,

as someone very serious once said,
what of murder, what of the bullet
worming red tunnels in flesh?
It's not that I want to carry one,

though sometimes it seems crazy not to,
it's that I can't ignore the gleam—
like birdsong—of light on the barrel,
and on my friend, taste it, her smile.

## OLD CYPRESS OF THE BLACK

To have watched the pin oak, because wet, burn slower than the birch;

to have felt the teal's every roost
at the margin of twilight's last shard,
to have had & to have held,

to have seen beneath the bark the wood's harvests of sugar,
and heard it hiss, and smelled its kinship
to earlier stars;

to have marched forth, to have retreated

and then entrenched for years in love's holy war;

we came to a place where the leaves
did not care for us anymore

than the returns. There

we stayed, two birds,
flitting among the fallen limbs.

❧

Two wood ducks on a westward beam,
the sky a laminate,
a low ceiling—there
was ease again. We had no words
for the standing by. Was a burn.
Was toothmarks
on the cypress knee. Nobody spoke
of black sand or of smoke
from the fire
where February laid

its hands, gave another fragrance
to the rain
that we darkened with beans
and sipped by the bank watching the beavers
go like need
this way & that.

❧

All blemish & swarth, the bottom
wasn't far,
          was sand, roots, blowdown.
What underwater
mistletoe grew? Nuthatch
in Spanish beard.
Low February sun in every face that lived
in or on the trees. A hard breeze, a harder stillness
to undo. The canoe far
too red & long. This way was fine.
That way was okay, & grew.

❧

A dark translucence
of cinnamon: how the openings began
to swallow us
               slower. Heron,
kingfisher, titmouse. Nothing dramatic,
yet a gulf of minnows,
          every edge,
a feathering of needles,
      bay leaf, tupelo,
in the loam.

❧

To the edge of edgelessness we slid.
Even the turning had learned
to spill. Land again
like a disappointment.

The channels came together again.
There was no way
in the now unbridled sunlight
but out of cypress

to be hewn.

❧

The river, without teeth, was darkly tongue.

We meant to stay under forever.
Life had rarely felt
so ribboned,
so what.

❧

Two thousand years.
After that, things got tidal fast.
There were naps involved. There were children.
Another shoreline.
The wind gave us hell.
The ocean couldn't stay put.

## SANDBAR, EARLY JUNE, KANSAS RIVER

Something in the water smells like a dead zone. Something
    in the mud creeps across my heel.

You can drift out here. The silt, the silt. Every dust bowl longs
    to be soup. I mean the sky

is totally Sanskrit,
    and flycatcher's still working that little willow's atmosphere

like he owns the place, like
    even the cottonwoods have quit giving the wind

some lip. I love near-island's bluffsheer, that loaf of loess look.
    Go on, Mama Kaw,

dredge me. Silver maple, show me some leg.
    There's an eagle now. Of course there's a fucking eagle. I mean

upwellings so perverse
    one longs to strike a match. And vultures, just upstream, steady

at conjugating carp into kite frame. God,
    you old trotliner, I'm going to clean all your hooks

and then make a necklace, lots of necklaces, from what cordage,
    what sinkers. For nowhere, its throat.

## EAST OF SUNDAY

But soilsmells, a gleam
unscarleting—

these are expected now,
nearly. So the fleeting infinities—

young maple vine-coiled, still
in leaf. A glimpse of silence, and at night

the same. For now,
snail on logrot, needled duff—

home a little sun
in the face, earfuls of birdsurf.

~

Mist in the overstory, mist in the under,
and light through it
                                        and on the silklines it shines,
stringy & tracered. Groggy is good,
and fatigue, and that dull edge that might
be waking.
Consider the poplar, the one
behind you, the only one, its splotchwork
                    of sun here & there,
there more than here.

~

I'm sitting on a vintage timber,
amazed beyond feeling.

Kiss me, says the coreopsis.
So I do.

Still this din of crickets & Mexican radio.
Bathtub, cement mixer,

Port-a-john. After all,
October's a morning of afternoons,

Wednesday for seven days.
It takes a pillage.

~

Forget the sweetgum leaves with their long faces,
the pollen fronds of the yellow pine.

For now, it's sap smells vaguely cinnamon,
it's crackers & humus,
phantasmal chit chat,
the ascension of a smile.

~

Acorned & gnomic, trees, too, are mists.
Candles of.

Believing's almosts.
Who says flame dives
into burn. Utterly, as when key words dissolve

in love's database—hickory's flares,
nonetheless of pines. Yondering pine. So October
is a server

going down. Ordinary gaze,
ordinary orbit. Blanks. A sky of many. Dew.

❧

And how (sliding through us—no cascade,
no breaks or rips
or falls), how
decadence, bivalved &
Bionicled, unzips us, here

among frescoes of frost on leaves,
some extinction—auk, mastodon—

rewound. Blanched
I mean, nearly green with gnaw.

# AT POPHAM BEACH

Haze of wave spume towards Small Point,
  Seguin Island Light like a whale's spout—
maybe life washes itself here, cools off.
  It never comes clean. See all the sails up
and full in the windy parade of skin
  and sand & brine. Soon the rocks will pluck
each wave's feathers. Soon the beach
  like the moon, waning, will be 1/8th its size.
Somewhere else—maybe Ireland—the tide
  will bottom out then. For now the sun
blesses the bodies at home in theirs,
  and those less so, to ruin & ruin's aftermath—
whatever that is—and the waves rolling in,
  little snowplows, nimbus in miniature; how
the beach fishhooks east, one child—
  is that mine, or some spirit I was one more
usher of?—face up, arms & legs
  scraping a temporary angel in the sand.

# AS WE WERE, THEN, ON THOSE STEEPS: OCONEE BELL

*S. galacifolia* was judged to be in a relict condition with the low incidence ofreproduction sites accounting in part for its endemism.
*V.E. Vivian, 1967*

In June 1760...Montgomery quickly drove the enemy from about Fort Prince George and then, rapidly advancing, surprised Little Keowee, killing every manof the defenders, and destroyed in succession every one of the Lower Cherokee towns...
*James Mooney, 1889*

A lot of plant distribution is logical; the rest is luck and history that we don't understand.
*L.L. Gaddy, 2016*

*–1760*

Runner-stem by runner-stem, the sisters
unstitched us from the duff: leaf, flower, root
and all. June, Green Corn Moon, it was,
*De ha lu yi*, and we were in capsule, mute
as ever while the two maidens bent, fingers

still quivering, numb with numb, and tore
us up from the ground in long strands (what
you might now call stolons), and with us
wrapped every corpse—there were a lot.
The younger gave her father extra care:

covered his eyesockets with our sepals,
braided dense his head with our toothed
leatheries, filled his mouth with our tongues—
styles, pollen tubes done, song-sleuthed.
They could smell smoke & strange metals

from across the river beyond the confluence,
the fort's wasteful, ridiculous fires,
but they worked as ghosts, quiet as
ghosts (though fox-screams were their eyes),
and *Nunne'hi* guided them, those Immortals lent

them strength of mist. Bees had spread the news.
Deer came to bed in our last dense clumps.
To settle their guts, bear munched our leaves,
turkey, too, but not excessively (our juice
has little taste). Scavengers, normally aloof,

flared their wings and cocked their heads, bald
and painted, up from their rank, perfect food.
From Spear-point's peak, Thunderbird, abuzz,
tucked & dove along the vectors of our nod.
Even the wolves left watch of the cattle

by the fort, and slunk to the top of the cliff
and stared down the slope at the sisters
who had woven the entire grove of us
by now around their kin. It wasn't over.
The deads' wounds mostly hidden (not the stiff

weight), the sisters hefted each villager,
family & friends, one by one to the stream.
And one by one down the sisters weighed
each runner—and leaf-entwined remain
with stones they tilted under the water,

big stones, boulders—such was the force
of their loss. For a long time (that felt
like none or beyond time), the sisters
worked the pool beneath the last tumult
at *Dukus'i*, Toxaway, before the confluence—

they waded among murmurs of light & rains
breaking on (and, more slowly, breaking)
the stone; those falls below which some say
every beforelife's future is spoken, and one
can know us as we are beyond the names.

# OUTWATER

Olivewhite with morning sun, the creek
is ribbon candy.
                                        Sit down, it says.
Among bloodstone.
See in seep's mud where black bear stepped.
Listen to the jewelweed
as it hums an orange grace.

❧

It's bugthirst & big trees—
basswood, poplar, oak. And burls
like gargoyles. And maybe despair once rooted here.
How else the wind bearing news
                                                                        of the gorge,
its breakier reaches:
millipedes, cascades, trillium gone to fruit.

❧

Pulse, maybe, or maybe
                                                        body, how bulbs
of rhododendron blossoms begin
to open. Look here, under the laurel's last snow,
where softness grows softer:
furtherings –
seed of the lily, seed of the breeze.

❧

Now the canopy bleeds
evening. Light like vastness puddles.

Updraft,
          where deadfall crocodiles
and bark slows to the scripture of being,
time's toadlike—it breathes you,
it pours you out.

❧

Whatever bugs in sun say with their glide,
there's branchwork—knoll, confluence, nest—
in every breath, a limb,
a lambency, and maybe blossoms
still tremor in creekwind,
that stuff of collisions,
                              of outwater, of in.

❧

Rootgrasp. Curve & nook. See
the bark's fretwork. Things bulbous,
flayed. Yes,
               the leaves weather.
Yes, drainage goddess licks them up.
Call it a whorled.
Spell it as you like.

❧

Laddersplash, waves
in wrungs. Here giving means
letting in.
Consider the sieve,
                         peeled log hung
in nape. All the bughover.
Thrushthroat liquid & trill.

❧

So the other world is this, the one
one slows to know.
Nothing new. No
hurry in the stones. No gongs in the trees—
all's trance, all's shiver.
And in the stalks—their slightness,
their give.

# MUSSELS

Plucked from ledge, from water below
lowest tide, and stowed in mesh
lashed to the stern;

we eat them now, steamed in brine,
succulent nubbins, tongues not our own.
As much for ritual as appetite,

the foraging, there's health in that.
*Like eating the sea, a distillation—*
we're licked towards breathing, towards

the tides that turn, yet you ask,
you have to, why the ones
that never open nourish us most.

## HORIZON NOTES

Two shrimp boats on the horizon, two gulls above them.
                    Glassy morning, the surf milk & butter:
a bit of sea oat, a hint of bonemeal.

☙

I'm partial to the shallows today,
          their tern-punctured margins & archipelagos
of spume,
      their depths.

☙

Out there my brother's learning to surf.
He's holding a yellow longboard,
pelican above him & haze.
He's looking out.

☙

And suddenly (& maybe always)
everything is rinse.
                    Or strafe.
I mean it's colorless nearly.
Very glare.

☙

                         No plants, no shells—
the breeze is loud & the sky is dry.
Even the sand has tan lines. Call it rockstuff,
          Edisto's load.

I'm closer to thinking
that life is an illusion now—
bleached sky, the water
a tired green—closer

but not that close.

Six hundred million years ago, they say
the horseshoe crab walked here,
eating as it walked,
only when it walked,
chewing food—as it chews it now—
with its legs; four eyes,
gills breathing

oxygen, water; blood
turning blue in the air.

Midday, wind from the east, swimmers
getting small
as the tide falls.
Two lines—

sand & water, water & sky.
Betweens. Not a cloud, nor a hint of one.

Waves like mopheads
this afternoon, mushy & awash, whitecaps
beyond them,
of them. And there, while we swim
again—as if we never didn't—
another kite
stalls & lifts, banks, spins
in lively translations of wind.

# LITTLE REED CREEK

Here's about to, the prepwork,
saprise & seepdrip. Here
is all there
isn't to know.

~

Schisms in the soilsphere—
toothwort, violet, cleaver.

~

Early April,
poplar's green shiver,
visibility for glades.

~

This ridge Terrapin Mountain,
that one, White Oak Knob—
no morels yet, many ferns still curled.

~

Plungepools & pocketwater—
trillium there, & there, trillium.

~

Don't call it work
what the boulders do,
but what they don't do, the rest.

The punchbowls, the hollows in every hollow.

❧

              Here is lair, and the waterthrush
at evening piping up,
                                        at morning, too.

❧

Still a little bite in the air,
still a little gobbler scratch, & rue.

❧

              The duff a treatise on parchment,
weather's imprint,
                                  notes on the future,
the last next generation all at once.

❧

        Buckrub & split trunk, a tick in your flanksteak,
deadfall, more deadfall.
                                        If zest, if spritz.

❧

That it go on, the hellebore,
the black birch's shelf life,
        polypore & parasitic burls.

❧

Anemone, anemone.

# LINES FROM THE CHALKBOX

Reprise of leaf slap & leaf drip.
                    Such is summer. Don't say the end
is a bright light. Don't say it is a mist

like a halo over the earth.
It's just another afternoon shower,
          the sky remodeling itself.

ঌ

Maybe the clouds are joists and space
is an attic. Or do you prefer to think in adobe
this time of year? Mud,
wood—all's runoff,
that's all, silt.

ঌ

Cedar knotty & lavender,
mullein in full swell—
                              I'm centered
by the edge of things:
shark's fin of granite, the tassels on its lichen,
all the splotches & unmown sides.
Who knows
                if there's an amen

like the vines, who knows
about the little economies. It's here
I cling to, the milky cosmos

of clover. Here, catching the deliveries

when they come. They come.

❧

Butterfly in the slag
                                        of the cement truck's chute.
Cinderblocks, a tarp
sun-bleached & stained,
some droneon the radio. Look,

the siding's up. It's cloudy.
But even the heart
is passive solar. Consider the stud-ends
beneath the chopsaw,
                                        so many quarters,
so many sixteenths.

❧

The day is of two minds—
rain & sun. Or maybe all afternoons are schizo. Ask the tick, the
fatty keeping watch
                                        on the dog's forehead—
                              it might take its meal according to thunder,
as if vibrations tripped its switch,
               the way certain movies give the rain
another layer of falling. Beneath

the butterfly's path even.
There it comes, here it goes.

❧

Light in hashmarks, shadows in them, too.
Quiet summer morning.

The birds are quiet. The trees are quiet.

I've been binge praying, but I've been quiet.
And suddenly I know there's a proper amount
of wickedness in the world,
                                        and it, too, though often loud,
is quiet.

~

First quarter moon, Jupiter
          a little to the left
and down, storms on it
                    large enough to devour Earth.
Meanwhile, in the rafters, a carpenter bee,
fuzzy star, chews its way into spruce.
It's hum is an orbit. It's orbital, I mean.
Now Puccini
                    on the jambox
reinvents nymphood, and the electrician,
tattoo of an anchor halfway
out the sleeve of his polo shirt,
rolls his eyes.

~

Dervishes off the chopsaw,
mud dauber in the backfill
that's vermilion & damp
                                        with last night's rain.
*Plumb this, snap a line.*
*Put a brace on the gable end.* Yes,
a universe of particle board,
bored particles.
                    Stellar dust.

# WEARY WAS NOT THE WORD FOR THAT PLACE

You found a land where names for things
were left alone.
                    The people there, the animals & plants
& stones,

they welcomed you anyway
with elegant indifference. And besides

you gave them names. You resisted their refusals.
It was pleasant

learning to worship refusal.

❧

Arrival was endless, for instance.
And

it was a late time, a tarnished season.
Little melodies, little rain.
                                        And then

the rain arrived,
the era of the end of leaves,
the nights all recurve & flint.

❧

In that land, hauling sacks of names
you pitched a tent,
a dome of breath,
                    by forty-seven streams,

and slept outside of it.

A small tent, of course, and the sacks

they needed to stay dry.

ঌ

There were other ways to be embraced.
You had to fall on your face once in a while.
            Everything pelvic & potluck,
everything goblinate—fanaticism

no longer came to mind,
the land so fully inhabited it. Yes,

the land there—& all the things upon it—
were tired of reaching for the sky.

ঌ

You studied the hemlocks.
You saw them losing needles, growing out

of touch with their roots.
They tried being

bridges for squirrels, perches
for heron. Some blamed it

on adelgids. Others blamed it on greed.
The adelgids were thriving, it was clear,
as much as the others,
                                    the lovers of blame.

ঌ

How bemused the owls remained,
          the few that remained,

and shy.
You took one
                    for stock—talon, skull, beak.
All night it simmered.
Later
you courted forever on the wilds of such drink,

for a while,
          a slow while & tremoring
and prior to anything resembling a name.

# ACCORDING TO SAND

I'm staring down the ghost crab's periscope.

The day is much stemmed, the day's a shadow puppet.
Sea oats, sea oats & Spanish bayonet.
Between the beneaths
                                        —you know how it is—

slender, thick stemmed splendor.

~

This. This is a beach at sunup
                                                  on a tide so low

it must be running from something—
I'm going to friend it, track its skidmarks & squiggles—

cave paintings, sedimentologies—
and see what the plover
                                          posts on its wall.

~

White spaces, constellations of crumble,
                                                            crumble & surge
margin & trundle. I never had a mind

for righteousness, never had a mind at all,
just a bunch of waves

                                        and one or two ways
to duck under, ride them.

❧

Trough to peak, the usual correspondences—
but more Dramamine, more peach
unbluing. Crow over dunes,

the dunes a thicket of thickets.
                                        The sun's up
to its usual banditry—nice,
a bit sweaty. There go three pelicans.

❧

And there: two shrimp boats way out there.
A little windswell, piddly mush—

sweet & lazy song. So it goes. The myrtle,
the bay leaves.
                    Deer paths in dunes.

The ocean felting its pearly wool.

❧

Barrier islands bury our eyes.

It's a long way to supportive,
to suppertime.
                    A blessed, balmy way.

The waves, larger or smaller,
they say hush, they sound like rest.

# ACKNOWLEDGMENTS

Many thanks to the editors of the following publications in whose pages some of these poems first appeared, sometimes in slightly different form:

*Birmingham Poetry Review*: "Father on the Beach, Tide Coming In"
Cerise Press: "Figure Drawn on the Ground as the Bull Moose Urinates Upon Waking,""According to Sand," and "Weary Was Not the Word for that Place"
*Conte*: "From the Bow and the Stern"
*Field*: "Old Dog," "Lines from the Chalkbox" and "Shadow"
*Hampden-Sydney Poetry Review*: "West Fork of the Little" and "Little Reed Creek"Off the Coast: "Fog Mull"
*Open City*: "Mussels"
*Orion*: "Sandbar, Early June, Kansas River"Poetry: "At Popham Beach"
*Taproot*: "As We Were, Then, On Those Steeps"Tarpaulin Sky: "Dix Island Serenade"
*Terrain*: "Old Cypress of the Black"
*The Southern Review*: "Thaw"
*Virginia Quarterly Review*: "Cold Range, Hot Range"Verse: "The August Listener"
*West Branch*: "Taking it Easy, Taking it Slow"

"Thaw" was reprinted in *A Face to Meet the Faces: An Anthology of Contemporary Persona Poems* (University of Akron Press, 2015); "On Hearing the Waterthrush Again, Jefferson" first appears in *Monticello in Mind: Fifty Contemporary Poets on Jefferson* (University of Virginia Press, 2016); and "As We Were, Then, On Those Steeps" appears in *A Literary Field Guide to Southern Appalachia* (University of Georgia Press, 2019). Much gratitude to the editors of those publications.

Great thanks, as always, to my family, to my friends, and to my students and colleagues at Hollins University.

# ABOUT THE AUTHOR

Thorpe Moeckel is director of the Jackson Center for Creative Writing at Hollins University. He is author of seven books, including *Watershed Days* and *Down by the Eno, Down by the Haw: A Wonder Almanac.* The recipient of many awards and fellowships for his writing, Moeckel lives around Roanoke, where he loves to explore the good woods, waterways, and ridges of Virginia and West Virginia. Learn more about him at www.thorpemoeckel.com.